A Practical Treatise on the Culture of the Dahlia

by Joseph Paxton, FLS HS

with an introduction by Roger Chambers

This work contains material that was originally published in 1903.

This publication was created and published for the public benefit, utilizing public funding and is within the Public Domain.

This edition is reprinted for educational purposes and in accordance with all applicable Federal Laws.

Introduction Copyright 2018 by Roger Chambers

Self Reliance Books

Get more historic titles on animal and stock breeding, gardening and old fashioned skills by visiting us at:

http://selfreliancebooks.blogspot.com/

Introduction

I am pleased to present yet another title on Gardening.

The work is in the Public Domain and is re-printed here in accordance with Federal Laws.

As with all reprinted books of this age that are intended to perfectly reproduce the original edition, considerable pains and effort had to be undertaken to correct fading and sometimes outright damage to existing proofs of this title. At times, this task is quite monumental, requiring an almost total "rebuilding" of some pages from digital proofs of multiple copies. Despite this, imperfections still sometimes exist in the final proof and may detract from the visual appearance of the text.

I hope you enjoy reading this book as much as I enjoyed making it available to readers again.

Roger Chambers

CONTENTS.

	PAGE
INTRODUCTION—	
First introduction of the plant	7
Derivation of name	9
Where indigenous	11
Different species	ib.
Rapid progress in its cultivation	12
Colours	13
EASY CULTURE—	
Some sorts more easily cultivated than others	18
EFFECT OF CLIMATE AND SOIL—	
Warm climate most favourable	19
Soil more influential than climate	ib.
Amelioration of uncongenial soils	20
Indigenous soil	21

CONTENTS.

	PAGE
Objectionable soils, and why so	21
Errors respecting rich soil	22
Flowers diminished and impoverished by too rich soil	23
This rule generally applicable	23
Constant moderate moisture about the roots necessary	ib.
Great moisture injurious	24
To correct wet clayey soil	ib.
To correct light friable soil	27
To correct light soil lying above pure clay	28
To correct intermediate soils	29
Different opinions respecting the most congenial soils	30
Difference of soil for dwarfs and fine plants	32
Moderation in manure essential to produce fine plants	ib.
Wonderful effects of cultivation as exhibited in the Dahlia and Heartsease	33
Experiments in culture highly useful	34

SITUATION—

Requires a free open situation	37
Delights in the sunshine	ib.
Native locality, *open plains*	38
Preferable aspects	39

CONTENTS.

	PAGE
Moderate elevation of the Dahlia bed above the surrounding surface, advantageous	39
Open sloping border best adapted to display the flowers	40
Distance between the roots	ib.

PROPAGATION—

To propagate the old and known varieties	42
To force the shoots	43
To remove the shoots	43
Mr. Glennie's method	ib.
Another method of starting the plants	44
The shoots must be kept short and strong	ib.
The roots to be thrown away when enough cuttings are taken	45
Potting the shoots	ib.
Shade necessary on first potting	ib.
Air and light requisite	46
When to shift into larger pots	ib.
Root grafting	47
Inferior sorts answer for Stocks	ib.
Blake's method of root grafting	48
Nash's method	50
Propagating in open beds	51
Another method	53
Whether or not heat is desirable in propagating	54

CONTENTS.

	PAGE
Propagation by summer cuttings	56
Propagation by autumn cuttings	57

PLANTING OUT—

Mr. Sabine's directions as to the effect of colours and size	59
Distance between the roots and rows in beds	60
Distance between the roots in avenues	ib.
Distance between the roots when grown for competition	ib.
Period for planting out	62
Care in transferring from pots to beds	ib.
Subsequent attention	63
Best time for watering	64
Precautions in extreme heat	ib.
Attendant disadvantages	65
On the use of manure water	66

PRODUCTION OF VARIETIES—

By seed	67
To procure good seed	68
Artificial impregnation	69
Time for sowing	70
Manner of sowing	ib.
Potting	71
Shifting	ib.

CONTENTS.

	PAGE
Treatment as for cuttings	71
Opinions respecting the analogy of colours in the stems and flowers	ib.
To ascertain the colours	73
Necessity of checking the bloom when the colour is ascertained	74

TRAINING—

General mode	77
Trimming for a bushy head	78
Limiting the number of blossoms	ib.
Attention to time necessary in trimming, &c.	79
Unfair means employed in public exhibitions	ib.
Shading from the sun and rain	81
Training with three stakes	82
Training in iron frames and stands	83
Training as espaliers	84
Training by pegging down the shoots	85

PRESERVATION OF ROOTS—

Time for digging up	89
Protection of roots previous to digging	ib.
Digging and dressing	90
Materials in which to preserve dry and dormant	91
Atmosphere and temperature	ib.
Place	92

CONTENTS.

	PAGE
Mr. Loudon's plan of preserving the roots	93
Old mode of preserving in pits and cellars	95
Objections thereto	96
Method of preserving in the open air	ib.

CHARACTERISTICS OF EXCELLENCE—

Comprised in three particulars	99
Characteristics of a fine blossom	100
Rules for judging of flowers	ib.
Three tests	101
Form	102
Colour	105
Size	106

CONCLUSION—

Numbers of sorts now in cultivation	108
Price of new sorts	109
Gradual reduction in price from year to year	ib.

INTRODUCTION.

No occupation is more worthy of an intelligent and enlightened mind, than the study of Nature and natural objects; and whether we labour to investigate the structure and functions of the human system, whether we direct our attention to the classification and habits of the animal kingdom, or prosecute our researches in the more pleasing and varied field of vegetable life, we shall constantly find some new object to attract our attention, some fresh beauties to excite our admiration, and some previously undiscovered source of gratification and delight. But, perhaps, if we range through the whole territory of nature, and endeavour to extract from each department the rich stores of knowledge and pleasure they respectively contain, we shall not find a more refined or purer source of amusement, or a more interesting and unfailing subject for recreation, than that which the observation and examination of the structure, affinities, and habits of plants and vegetables, affords. In this study (to use the words of an eminent writer) " all is elegance and delight. No painful, disgusting, unhealthy experiments or inquiries are to be made. Its pleasures spring up under our feet, and, as we pursue them, reward us with health and serene satisfaction."

As a proof of this, we need only refer to the present state of the science of botany, and we shall find, that, as the mind of man becomes more enlightened; as each succeeding age attains to a higher standard of intelligence; as the "march of intellect" advances with rapid and precipitate strides, dispelling the dark clouds of ignorance and prejudice; as man takes an additional delight in cultivating his mental powers, and approaches nearer to the apex of intellectual refinement,—the science of horticulture (in connexion with botany) becomes increasingly studied, and is every day gaining large accessions to the list of its devoted admirers. This affords a most gratifying evidence, that it is one of the most delightful and rational occupations in which the human mind can be engaged, and gives us just and reasonable grounds for supposing, that it has yet a much higher degree of perfection to attain, inasmuch as our knowledge of it is yet exceedingly limited. Not only is the science of horticulture now studied with a view to the attainment or aggrandisement of pecuniary wealth; not only do we find the gardener devoting his attention and energies to it for the sake of obtaining a maintenance,—but from the retired tradesman and gentleman to the most influential nobleman, and even with ladies of the highest rank and first distinction, this study has now become a favourite pursuit; and all are aiming, according to their several stations and means, to promote and increase their knowledge of, and acquaintance with, this most interesting subject.

Under these circumstances, while innumerable works are constantly issuing from the press, replete with directions for arranging and cultivating the various tribes, the author of the following pages has observed with regret, that, while no plant or tribe of plants is more worthy of attention than the Dahlia, as far as he is aware, no work has ever yet appeared expressly and exclusively devoted to the subject of its cultivation; and he feels convinced, that he is only expressing the sentiments of the great majority of the community, when he says, that he has for some time past been anxiously looking for the publication of such a work. In this expectation, however, he has hitherto been disappointed, and this alone has induced him to take upon himself the task, which otherwise he would most gladly have seen performed by other and more competent individuals; but, resting his claim to notice entirely on the experience which he has acquired from many years' successful practice in the cultivation of this plant, he confidently introduces this little work to the attention of an indulgent public, without the slightest doubt of its being favourably received. Should he, however, in this respect be disappointed, he will still possess the gratifying reflection, that he endeavoured to promote and extend the cultivation of a plant of which he has long been a most ardent admirer, and in the management of which such extraordinary improvements have been effected in so short a space of time.

In tracing the history of this plant, from the era of its introduction into this country to the present period, and considering the progress that has been made in its cultivation during that time, I cannot but arrive at the conclusion, that the state of perfection to which it has already attained is absolutely unparalleled in the history of any other plant or tribe of plants at present known to our collections; and perhaps I shall not be guilty of a departure from truth when I say, that it is at present by far the most interesting, beautiful, and popular autumnal-flowering plant, of which the gardens of this country can boast.

No plant, or tribe of plants, of the most acknowledged beauty, or the most extensive variety of form and colour, has ever excited so much interest and attention, or been so successfully and universally cultivated by British florists or horticulturists, as the one here noticed; and we have no difficulty in accounting for this, when we take into consideration the low price for which the most esteemed sorts may be obtained, and reflect on the extreme ease and facility with which new varieties may be raised, and old ones cultivated and perpetuated; besides which, the almost endless diversity and variety of the colours of its flowers, their elegant form, the great profusion in which they are produced, and the brilliant and rich display exhibited by them when expanded, have severally and unitedly contributed to obtain for the Dahlia such universal admiration and esteem, and to cause its eager and extensive cultivation to amount almost to a mania.

We are informed from indisputable authority, that this plant was first introduced into this country from Spain, by the Marchioness of Bute, so early as 1789; but, as it was not subsequently heard of, it is supposed to have been lost shortly after this introduction.

In 1804, accounts are recorded of seeds of this plant having been transmitted by Lady Holland, from the Royal Garden at Madrid, to Mr. Buonaruti, then resident in this country. From these seeds a few plants were produced, and some of them flowered in the following season; while two others are said to have flowered in the garden of Lord Holland in the autumn of the second year.

From this period to the year 1814, the cultivation of the Dahlia made very little progress with us, although during this time it had been most successfully cultivated in the Royal Gardens of Spain, France, and Germany; and from thence *roots* of several varieties were imported into this country. After this time, (1814,) the Dahlia was introduced to more general notice, and cultivated in most collections; but it was reserved for the intelligent cultivators of the last few years to circulate it more extensively, and make the most rapid advances towards a state of perfection. Indeed, so lately as eight or ten years since, it was considered a perfectly novel sight, to witness Dahlias with double flowers in the garden of a tradesman or cottager; but, owing to the astonishing rapidity with which new and good sorts have since been obtained and circulated, it is now quite as rarely that we see or meet with a cottager's garden, which does not contain at least a few good Dahlias; and many possess plants of first-rate sorts.

The botanical name, *Dáhlia*, was first given to this genus in honour of Dahl, a Swedish botanist, by Cavanilles, a Spanish botanist;

but the propriety of this having been disputed on account of its resemblance to *Dalea*, a name previously bestowed on a genus of a totally different nature; and more especially as the name of the genus under consideration is frequently, but vulgarly, pronounced *Dàylia;* many botanists agreed to change the name to *Georgina*, some say in honour of Georgi, a Russian traveller and botanist, while others assert, in compliment to Lady Holland, through whom it was introduced into this country: but, although the learned M. de Candolle and other eminent botanists adopted the latter appellation, and although many efforts have been made to establish it in this country, it has been found that the original name, *Dáhlia*, had become too generally known and received to be easily eradicated; besides which, having the priority of publication, (which is considered conclusive in such matters,) it is now almost universally acknowledged.

The Dahlia is a native of the high sandy plains of Mexico, where it was first discovered by that eminent and indefatigable botanist, Humboldt, 5000 feet above the level of the sea, but in what year we have no authentic accounts. There are three distinct species of this genus; *D. coccinea*, *D. Cervantesii*, and *D. variabilis*; of which the two former are not now cultivated, as they do not readily sport into varieties, and are much less beautiful than *D. variabilis*, from which latter, all the innumerable varieties at present known to our collections have emanated.

From the most authentic sources we thus learn that the Dahlia has been cultivated in this country for upwards of thirty years; but perhaps, during the whole of that time, it cannot strictly be said to have attained any degree of perfection till within the last ten years; and, if we take a retrospective view of the progress of Dahlia culture during this brief period, what abundant cause have we for wonder and astonishment! each succeeding year produces some fresh beauties to admire; each revolving season develops some new peculiarities of shape and colour; every annual catalogue apprises us of immense accessions to our previous stock; and we are involuntarily led to exclaim, " Where will all this terminate?" but, to this interrogatory, time alone can afford a solution; and, whatever conjectures may be entertained, it is impossible to come to any satisfactory conclusions.

We may, indeed, reasonably infer, from what the last few years have shown; from the high state of perfection to which this plant has been brought; from the long experience we have had with respect to its habits, and consequently the system of cultivation most congenial to them which we have thence been enabled to deduce,—that, in the course of a similar space of time, we shall have Dahlias of almost every variety of form, and nearly every shade of colour; but, that we shall ever grow the flowers much larger than we do at present, is a matter of great doubt and uncertainty.

M. de Candolle, in his essay on the genus, alludes to the improbability of a blue Dahlia ever being produced, as he considers the fundamental and radical types of the colours of flowers to be blue and yellow; these colours, therefore, mutually exclude each other; and though yellows pass readily into red or white, they never change to blue; blue flowers also frequently change to red or white, but never to yellow. But it is not unreasonable to imagine, that, ere long, we shall have Dahlia flowers containing infinite combinations of those rich, clear, and exquisitely beautiful colours, for which the tulip has been so long and deservedly admired; perhaps, ere long, our fancy may be gratified by seeing Dahlias with the two opposite shades of black and white, associated in striking contrast in one flower; perhaps, ere long, Dahlia flowers will be produced, vying in beauty and combination of hue with the choicest Carnation; perhaps, ere long, the popular taste may be captivated with flowers of a globular form, and we may then have Dahlias presenting the appearance of huge balls, of almost every variety of colour. Who would have conceived, some few years ago, that we should now have our tipped and our striped Dahlias of the most varied and striking combination of colour? Who would have supposed, that from one comparatively insignificant plant, such endless and innumerable beautiful varieties could have been produced? What will not the skill and ingenuity of man effect even in the vegetable world? and what may we not yet expect and anticipate? Only let cultivators persevere with the spirit they have manifested during the last few years;—let them be constantly alive to the subject of still further investigating and ascertaining the habits of this plant;—and, in the mean time, let them adopt those approved methods of cultivation which many years' experience has taught to be most suitable; but, above all, let them attend with increased assiduity to the production of new varieties, from seeds of the most esteemed sorts; and I feel assured, that the extent of perfection to which this handsome and favourite plant will ultimately be brought, will far exceed the most sanguine expectations of its most devoted admirers.

With these convictions, and as a means for promoting this most desirable purpose, being fully convinced that no improvement can possibly be effected unless due and proper attention is given to cultivation and management, I have been induced to bring the result of my own experience, and that of eminent practical men, before the public, in a compendious form, and at a price within the reach of all classes; and my only aim and desire is to advance and further the cultivation of a plant, than which a more splendid ornament, or a more decided acquisition to any collection, is not at present cultivated or known in British gardens.

Chatsworth,
March 12, 1838.

𝔄 Practical Treatise

ON THE CULTIVATION OF THE DAHLIA.

EASY CULTURE.

The cultivation of the Dahlia, without reference to the preservation of its roots during the winter, or to the various methods of propagation and multiplication in the spring, is perhaps attended with as little or less difficulty than that of any other ornamental plant we possess. As a proof of this, we need only direct attention to the gardens of nearly every cottager, tradesman, or nobleman; and, whether situated within the smoky precincts of the town, or in the purer and more salubrious atmosphere of the country, we scarcely ever fail to find this plant in the most perfect state of health, and almost as rarely destitute of its handsome and showy blossoms. This latter circumstance, however, depends more upon the sorts selected, than the soil or situation in which they may be planted; for some kinds produce their flowers much more freely and abundantly than others: still, while from one end of the country to the other, we seldom see or meet with an instance of failure in the cultivation of this plant, there is a degree of perfection which all are emulous of attaining, but which the greater number of growers seem wholly unable to reach; and which is only to be witnessed in the collections of a few zealous and persevering individuals, who, by experiments and investigation, have discovered the best methods of treatment.

EFFECT OF CLIMATE AND SOIL.

The majority of cultivators have, and I admit very reasonably, been inclined to attribute this superiority to the great variation of climate in different districts; for there can be little doubt that a warm and genial climate, like that of the south of England, possesses considerable advantages over the bleaker districts of the north; and so far favours the growth of this plant as almost invariably to give it a decided superiority, though under the same system of cultivation: but I do not believe that climate has such a material influence as is generally imagined; for I am firmly persuaded, that if more care and attention were bestowed with regard to situation and soil, the flowers produced in the north would be very little inferior to those raised in the south. Some may be disposed to regard this statement as rash and unfounded, and be ready to view the system I am about to propose for ameliorating the soil as too troublesome; magnifying the apparent labour required to carry it into effect to such an extent, as to lead them at once to reject it without a practical trial: not considering that the blossoms, by being so much finer, will make ample compensation for any extra labour bestowed; which indeed, in my estimation, is very trifling. I do not contend that the natural soil, however bad it may be, will require to be entirely removed, and its place supplied with fresh earth from a distance; but I do maintain, that the natural soil of any garden or other place, whether a stiff retentive clay, or a loose friable loam, may, by the admixture in due quantities of certain earths of different qualities, be so modified and adapted to the constitution of the Dahlia, that, if the cultivator's system of management in other respects is such as experience has shown to be most suitable, this, in conjunction with the ameliorated properties of the soil, will improve the characters of the flowers to a surprising extent. If we take into consideration the soil in which it is found indigenous, (*sandy pasture land*,) and which is consequently the most congenial to its habits, and compare it with the natural soil of most of the gardens and fields in England; we cannot do otherwise than allow, that the soil of nearly every district in this country is capable of being brought, with very little labour, to approximate in texture and quality to that which analogy and thirty years' experience have taught to be most favourable to the growth of this plant.

The soils I object to as being least adapted to the cultivation of the Dahlia are—first, that of a close texture, and wet, adhesive, retentive nature; and again, that which is light, without any disposition to bind, and containing an undue proportion of decomposed vegetable matter. All soils intermediate between these two extremes, may, with a trifling modification, be brought to that condition which I conceive to be most favourable to the culture of this plant. My reasons for objecting to the soil first mentioned, are—first, that in consequence of its wet close nature, it is too cold and cloggy about the tubers; and, in the second place, that it is too lean; and what little nutriment it does contain, is with such difficulty absorbed by the fibres or rootlets, as to be insufficient to enable the plant to develop properly all its parts. To the latter description of soil I object, on the ground of its being, in the first place, too porous; and, in dry weather, too liable to fail in retaining and supplying the necessary quantity of moisture: and, secondly, because it is too rich; in consequence of which the labours of the roots are lost in rank luxuriance, instead of being devoted to the uniform distribution of the nutritive principle through every part of the plant. It is a most fatal error to imagine that the flowers of Dahlias will be improved, or rendered larger, by being planted in a rich and highly nutritive soil; for instead of this being the case, they will expend all their strength in producing shoots and leaves, and the flowers will be few in number, and much impoverished; or they will be so rank and coarse, as to lose all that beauty of form which is so much desired in the Dahlia. Indeed, illustrations of this principle are by no means wanting in other plants; for what gardener is there who is not aware, that some plants require a soil in which there is but a very small portion of nutritive matter; and that, if they are placed in a rich soil, the result will be, that they will produce their flowers very scantily, and devoid of their proper character; or, in many instances, will not flower at all? Since then it is very clear that Dahlias are cultivated solely for the sake of producing fine and well-formed flowers, I think it is equally clear, that, if they are planted in a soil in which too much vegetable matter exists, and which is in consequence highly stimulating and nutritive, such treatment must be prejudicial to the formation and development of a great number of large and well-formed flowers.

As far as my observations (carefully made) enable me to judge with regard to the cultivation of the Dahlia, I always find that it thrives best when a medium quantity of moisture is retained about the roots; and that a perceptible deficiency invariably ensues, if the tubers are allowed to become saturated with, or imbibe more than a moderate degree of moisture; and the system I would suggest for reducing wet and clayey land to a due state of friability, is the following:—Early in the autumn, a heap of river or drift sand, and road scrapings (the former of which should preponderate) should be procured, and well incorporated by frequent turning: in this state it should, about the month of November, be taken to the land which it is intended to benefit, and spread equally over the surface, to the depth of about two inches: the land should then be subjected to the operation termed by gardeners *rough digging;* that is, every spadeful of earth should be turned over, so as to stand almost erect in an inverted position, and left as much unbroken as possible; and in this state remain exposed to the action of the wind and frost all the winter. Previous to digging it in the spring (March) strew another coat of the same compost (as before) all over the surface, to the thickness of two inches: this done, dig the whole carefully over, laying it as hollow as possible; so that its whole substance may receive the beneficial influence of the penetration of the air. In this condition it will be better to let it remain, till the time (May) arrives for planting out the Dahlias; when it may again be very superficially dug, or (as it is usually termed) *pointed* over: by this time the sand will have become in a great measure blended with the soil, and the land will be improved by this treatment to such a degree, as to be capable of being worked with comparative ease the following season: added to this, the Dahlias will grow to much greater perfection than before, the flowers will be far superior, and this improvement will become more obvious each successive year. After the first season, the land will be found to have become light, and have assumed an open friable texture; when it will be necessary to apply a small quantity of well-rotted manure of any description, in order to strengthen it. Of course, where the soil has been of a poor and barren, as well as stiff nature, a large proportion of manure will be required to render it at all nutritive; and I have no doubt that leaf soil, or that produced from decomposed small branches of trees, would be the best sort of manure for this purpose; as, while these would tend to enrich the soil, they would also assist much in rendering it light and friable. But where the soil has been rich and strong, as well as adhesive and stiff, manure should be very sparingly given, or wholly withheld until there is absolute necessity for it. This sort of soil, however, is by no means of common occurrence; and is seldom found where the land has been previously cultivated. By the practice of this system, I am persuaded that any stiff land may be so improved and ameliorated, as not only to enable it to grow good Dahlias, but almost any other herbaceous plant.

That a due proportion of moisture is necessary for the successful cultivation of this plant, is a fact too well known to require any argument to enforce it; and, consequently, soil that is too loose and open, will require some modification before it can be rendered capable of growing Dahlias to perfection; but the difficulty experienced in rendering friable land in any degree adhesive, is much greater than that of reducing adhesive land to a state of friability, as all must be aware. The means I have found most efficient for this purpose, have been to withhold manure for a few seasons, and after that, to apply only such a quantity of it as is absolutely necessary to afford sufficient nutriment to the crop I wished to obtain; and I am convinced, that land such as that now under consideration, may, with the exercise of a little skill and judgment in this respect, be brought to a good and proper state for the cultivation of the Dahlia, without impoverishing it to such an extent as to render it incapable of growing them of the best possible character, both as regards strong and well-formed plants, and also the number and beauty of their flowers. Besides this method, that of turning up the sub-soil from a considerable depth, that is, trenching it in the usual manner, is an excellent practice with land of this description, and will speedily render it adhesive and retentive. The practice of *trenching* is likewise highly advantageous where the soil has become exhausted; as by it manure may be dispensed with for a great length of time. But where the surface-soil is light and friable, and the sub-soil is composed of pure clay, (which is the case in some places in the vicinity of London,) another course must be adopted; and, instead of turning up the sub-soil, which would scarcely ever become incorporated with that of the surface, a quantity of strong maiden loam, taken from the surface of a meadow or common, with the turf attached, should be collected into a heap in the autumn, and suffered to remain in that state all the winter; excluded as much as possible from light, to promote the decomposition of the turf. In the spring it may be turned several times, and applied freely to the land in question; and this, in conjunction with the before-mentioned remedy of withholding manure, will soon render such land of a proper consistence for the purpose required.

In the above remarks it will be seen that I have noticed two exceedingly diverse soils; which, from their peculiar nature, are incapable of producing either plants or flowers so fine as the soil in which they are usually grown. I have endeavoured to show that the soil in both cases may be so far improved by the application of certain ingredients, and careful judgment in selecting and applying them, as to render it capable of growing Dahlias very little inferior to the best naturally suitable land. The condition of soils intermediate between the two extremes pointed out, may be improved and approximated to that which is here recommended as most suitable, in the following manner. When the surface-soil is more than moderately stiff, and the sub-stratum approaches to the consistence of clay, administer sand and other laxative ingredients, with well rotted manure in small proportions, as it may seem to require; and when the soil is too light and too rich, in digging it, let the spade sink over the shoulders of the blade, thus bringing a portion of the sub-soil to the surface, which will effectually improve it. In short, all that is necessary in this respect, is to practise either of the above systems in the manner and to the extent each may seem to require, and aim at converting the natural soil, as far as perseverance in the most approved means will allow, to the nature of an incorporated compound, consisting of moderately retentive, nutritive loam, and river sand, and I may likewise add, a little well-rotted manure.

I shall now quote the following authorities, with the view of laying before the reader the opinions of eminent practical men, who have written on the subject of the soil most suited to the constitution and habits of the Dahlia.

" Georginas (Dahlias) thrive best in rich loam, and a clear open space, neither sheltered by trees or walls. Like the potato, they exhaust the soil considerably, and do not thrive well when repeatedly planted in the same spot." *Loudon's Encyclopædia of Gardening, new Ed.* p. 1036.

" The soil best adapted for the growth of these plants (Dahlias) is a yellow rich loam; if recently taken from the pasture so much the better." *Dale, in Horticultural Register.*

The above authorities agree in considering that a loamy soil is the best for this plant, and sand is used more to promote drainage, where the natural texture of the soil is peculiarly stiff. Sand, I have no doubt, may also be employed with advantage, where the soil is too rich, or pregnant with vegetable substances in a state of decomposition; as it will tend to prevent that excessive luxuriance in stems and foliage always inimical to the production of good flowers. The soil obtained from decayed leaves may not only be employed in adhesive soils as a laxative, but also with advantage when the land is becoming exhausted, as it will restore its strength, without imparting those rank qualities, not essential, but rather detrimental, to the formation of good plants, and the development of an abundant display of fine flowers.

From the remarks thus submitted, the reader cannot fail to perceive what kind of soil a term of thirty years' experience has led practical men to recommend, as most adapted to the cultivation of the Dahlia. A very few years ago, the prevailing desire seemed to be to obtain dwarf plants, with a brilliant display of flowers exhibiting themselves above the branches and foliage; this, as is well understood, was only to be effected by growing the plants in a poor soil, mixed with an abundance of river sand; a practice not at all uncommon with plants that exhaust the earth merely for the production of leaves and branches. *Mesembryanthemums* for instance, if turned out into a very sterile soil, or pure river sand, generally flower abundantly. How very different is the aim of the cultivator at the present day! instead of dwarf plants, and a dazzling display of flowers merely because they are numerous, he manures to grow fine plants, and from fine plants he obtains flowers of merit, of a large size, regular shape, and beautiful symmetry in the form and dispositions of the petals.

I am, however, decidedly of opinion, that manure used in great quantities, is far from being beneficial; that it is useful in small quantities I readily grant, but administered too largely, I firmly believe that the main ends and objects of Dahlia culture are wholly counteracted. I have, in a former part of this treatise, stated my reasons for so thinking, and repeated experience convinces me that they are well

EFFECT OF CLIMATE AND SOIL. 33

grounded. It is well known, that the Dahlia is a native of the *sandy plains* of Mexico; and although I am not ignorant of the fact, that many plants have been wonderfully improved by cultivation, and that in this country some plants have been brought by high cultivation to surpass in size and beauty, plants of the same species found in their wild and native state, yet we must be cautious of departing too far from the precepts of nature, lest by attempting to improve we only deteriorate. Perhaps a more perfect instance of the extent to which cultivation may be carried, and the success with which it may be attended, is not to be found, than is presented to our view in the Heartsease; which, like the Dahlia, has risen within a few years from mere insignificance, to occupy a place in almost every garden; but we must by no means resort to precedent in nature, for in this respect she is perfectly ungovernable and erratic; and experience alone can teach what effect high cultivation will produce on any plant.

Let it not, however, be imagined from these re-

D

marks, that I am an enemy to investigation or experiment; for, on the contrary, I regard that individual as the greatest friend and patron of the science of floriculture, who most indefatigably exerts himself to ascertain what treatment is peculiarly adapted to any particular plant. But in this case, experience *has* shown that the Dahlia cannot be brought to deviate materially in its choice of soil from its natural habits, and that, if we once resort to very high cultivation, we may indeed obtain large, strong, and vigorous *plants;* but if we wish for good *flowers*, in great abundance, of perfect form, and rich and true colours, we must use a moderate, and only a moderate quantity of manure. I have already instanced the genus *Mesembryanthemum*, as supplying an illustration of this principle; and I might mention the genus *Œnothera*, most of the species of which only produce good flowers of their true colours in a very poor soil. But further illustration is here unnecessary, and if any of my readers are disposed to question the solidity of these assertions, I would recommend them to try the effect of high cultivation on this plant, and they will soon be convinced, that these opinions have not been delivered without mature deliberation and investigation.

Although at present only a few individuals eminent for their floricultural skill succeed in growing plants of the first order in merit, I feel a gratifying assurance, that in a few years every amateur and cottager will have, the former his pleasure-grounds, and the latter his strip of flower-border, decorated with Dahlias of the highest merit; for every individual, from the skilful and cunning florist and the nobleman's gardener, to the amateur and cottager, is striving, according to his particular circumstances and means, to arrive at a degree of perfection in the cultivation of this plant, far above what has at present been attained. Indeed, the return of every season surprises us with some additional beauty; and this gives me confidence in asserting, that the Dahlia will ultimately surpass in perfection any other flower that has ever engaged the attention of floricultural wisdom and skill; and what adds pleasure to the anticipation is, that it will not, like the

Tulip, &c., become only the aggrandising property of a few, whom Providence has favoured with riches and other means, whereby such plants alone can be procured; but it will become alike the property of the nobleman, amateur, tradesman, and cottager; every garden will boast of its Dahlia flowers, some possessing one feature of merit, and some another; and by this means, every town and village, and even our streets and houses, will be enhanced in interest, as the qualities of this flower are improved, and its beauties increasingly admired and appreciated.

SITUATION.

To proceed, however, to the subject of *situation*. Like most other border flowers, the Dahlia flourishes best in a situation, where it is neither subjected to the drippings from trees, nor shaded by them; and where its growth is not impeded or encumbered with other plants, either of its own or any other species. It delights in a position where it can constantly receive the vivifying and strengthening rays of the sun, from the time he issues forth in eastern glory, to the period of his setting below the western horizon. Indeed, the production of healthy plants, and consequently of good flowers, depends to so great a degree on the circumstance of their being planted in an open situation, that it becomes indispensably necessary that this particular should be duly and properly attended to. I do not intend to affirm, that Dahlias, when planted in the beds of the flower-garden, or the borders of the shrubbery, will not grow and flower so as to have a very ornamental effect, for, on the contrary, I have seen some very good flowers gathered from plants in such situations: but these cases can only be considered as exceptions, not as general rules; and I think no one will be found ignorant enough to contend, that a shaded and confined situation is most suitable for the cultivation of this plant.

In its native state, as I have before observed, the Dahlia is found growing on *open plains;* and from this, as well as many years' experience on the subject, we learn, that to grow this plant to perfection, it requires to be planted in a very open and exposed situation. To accomplish this important purpose, a large *flat*, or clear space of ground, should be selected; and particular care should be taken to choose a spot which lies open to the south, east, and west, so that the plants may receive the full benefit of the sun's influences: I mention these three aspects, because it is absolutely essential that they should remain exposed; whereas, it is quite immaterial whether the north side of the ground is or is not shaded. It is also important, that the situation chosen should not be in a low and excessively wet part of the garden; but, as far as practicable, above the level of the surrounding surface; as, though the former of these situations would ensure a more constant supply of moisture during the summer season, it would likewise much injure the tubers in the autumnal months, (which are very frequently rainy in this country,) by so completely saturating them with water, as to render it almost impossible to dry them sufficiently for preservation during the winter. It must not, however, be supposed that I am totally averse to the system of planting Dahlias in the borders of shrubberies, and other parts of the pleasure-ground; but, as by this practice the plants or flowers are never brought to a state of perfection, except in a few isolated instances, it is advisable that only the common and inferior sorts should be used for this purpose, and that those of the first class or order in merit be planted in beds or masses.

An excellent situation for planting them, and one which is well calculated to exhibit their flowers to the greatest advantage, is an open exposed border, which is raised (either naturally or artificially) at the back, and made to slope gradually towards a walk: in this position the flowers are presented to the eye in every variety of form; and, as the whole of the plants and blossoms may be seen at one view, the general effect produced is truly magnificent. In setting apart plants for this latter purpose, care should be taken to select the sorts of tallest growth for the rear of the border, and those which are of dwarfest stature for the front; filling up the intermediate space with plants of such an altitude, that, when they are in flower, the whole may form a gradual and uninterrupted slope from the back to the front of the border. In this situation they should be planted about two feet and a half distant from each other either way, leaving only sufficient room for the heads of the plants to expand, so as to occupy the whole of the intervening space when arrived at their full growth; and also for the more regular distribution of the flowers throughout the whole: it is also of primary importance that the sorts should be so arranged as to have a proper and pleasing admixture and variety of colours. When raised borders of this description lie parallel on each side of the walk, or have their margins judiciously and tastefully broken into irregular recesses, of from ten or twelve to three or four feet in depth, as well as the surface slightly and pleasingly undulated, and the whole planted with Dahlias selected with careful judgment, it is utterly impossible to describe the beauty and grandeur of their appearance, when the whole are in flower: and I am persuaded that not a richer, more brilliant, or more varied display of flowers could possibly be produced, from the combined beauty of any other family of plants in the whole field of vegetation.

PROPAGATION.

Having noticed the soil and situation best adapted to the cultivation of this plant, I shall now proceed to lay before the reader the method of propagation, which is very simple. This operation may be performed in various ways; and I shall first consider the measures to be adopted for propagating old and known varieties. About the latter end of February or the beginning of March, having prepared a bed of stable litter and leaves, and placed a frame and lights of the required size upon it, scatter over the surface of the bed a quantity of sandy mould and old bark, or partially decomposed leaves, to the depth of three inches; and if the steam which is produced by the fermentation is sweet and moderate, lay the roots on the above-named materials as closely as possible to each other; after which strew a little old bark or other light soil over them, observing not to cover the eyes. In this state they should be occasionally sprinkled with water that is partially warm; and if, after they are thus placed in the bed, a rank and dense steam arise, the lights of the frame should be slightly raised, both by night and day, till it subsides. This *gentle* bottom heat (if violent it almost universally causes the tubers to rot) will speedily induce the eyes to germinate; and when the shoots from them have attained the height of from three to four inches, they should be slipped or cut off close to the base, or, where they are abundant, they should always be taken off *with a portion of the crown attached**, which is a much more likely means of ensuring success. If a great stock of any particular kind is required, the cuttings should be taken off just below a joint, leaving the base of the shoot with one or two eyes to it; these

---

* Mr. Glenny's practice, when the eyes are plentiful, is to break the shoots off or out.

latter will speedily produce new shoots, which may again be removed in a similar manner.

Another method of starting the plants, is to place them in pots of a sufficient size, covering the roots with a light soil, and leaving the crowns exposed: then fill the pit of a vinery, or other forcing-house, with bark that has been previously partly exhausted, and in this state it will produce a mild and gentle heat: in this bark, plunge the pots containing the Dahlias up to the rim, and, with the heat derived from the bark, as well as that from the fires which are kept in the forcing-house, the eyes will soon begin to vegetate. This system possesses some advantages over the one before detailed; as by it the plants are kept distinct, and can be taken out and examined at any time, thereby affording greater facilities for taking off the cuttings. In either case, the plants should be kept as near as possible to the glass, that the shoots produced may be short, strong, and healthy; for if they are suffered to grow tall and weak, they will be exceedingly liable to damp off; or, if they do strike and live, will never make

PROPAGATION. 45

good plants. It is highly advisable that the roots from which the cuttings are taken, should be thrown away after the required quantity of young plants is obtained; as it is more than probable, that, if they are kept, they will not produce eyes in the succeeding season.

After the cuttings are taken off, pot them singly into small 60-sized pots, filled with light, open, sandy loam, and place them on boards on a moderate hotbed, or on the shelves of a hothouse, provided they are kept near the glass; for, as on the parent plant, so now, if they are suffered to be drawn and become weak, there will afterwards be a manifest deficiency in all their parts. After they are potted, each should receive a very moderate supply of lukewarm water, and great attention should be paid to shading them from the immediate influences of the sun; as, if they are once left exposed to its rays, they will seldom recover: in this state they should continue till they have formed their roots, which they will do in little more than a fortnight; during which period water should be administered sparingly and judiciously, observing not to wet the leaves, and not to keep the atmosphere of the house or frame too humid: air should also be admitted when the weather is fine, and the external atmosphere dry, and they should always have as much light as possible without being exposed to the direct rays of the sun; which, however, they may be gradually accustomed to after the first week is past, always remembering to cover them up at night with mats or other protection, unless the weather be decidedly warm. When the plants are rooted, they may be considered established; and all that is then necessary, is to shift them into pots of a larger size, as they may progressively require, and gradually inure them to a lower temperature, till they are able to endure the open air: this latter purpose may easily be effected, by placing them, first in a cooler frame, afterwards in a cold one, and finally exposing them to the natural atmosphere previously to planting them out; but this should not be done, without adopting every precaution to guard against bleak winds, or other adverse agents that may be likely to injure them while they are in so precarious a stage of their existence. Where frames or other conveniences are not at hand, for the purpose of forwarding the cuttings, or the reception of the young plants after they are rooted, potted, and become established, they may be placed in a light part of a dwelling-room where sufficient heat is maintained to exclude frost.

The preceding remarks, it will be seen, are restricted exclusively to what is termed " propagation by cuttings." I shall next consider that method of propagation by which plants are multiplied by grafting into the tubers. Root-grafting is very advantageous, when the sorts are very choice, and the cuttings weak or sickly; as plants which are raised in this manner, are ready for placing out much sooner than those produced from cuttings. Roots of any inferior sorts will answer perfectly well for stocks; and when the cuttings of the sorts intended to be propagated are in readiness, break off single tubers from the roots above named, and with a sharp knife slit them two inches downwards from the top, making the incision on one side only, and about half way through the tuber; then cut the end of the scion somewhat wedge-shaped, and insert it in the incision made in the tuber; after having bound the root round with good matting, pot it into a sixty-sized pot, and treat it in precisely the same manner as a cutting. As an excellent and detailed account of this mode of obtaining young plants, I insert the following from the *Hort. Trans.* vol. iv. p. 476, by Blake, to whom we are indebted for the first account of this system of propagation in this country.

" The cutting intended for the graft should be strong, and short-jointed, having on it two or more joints or buds; it must be also procured as soon in the season as possible; when obtained, select a good tuber of a single sort, taking especial care that it has no eyes; with a sharp knife (for a dull edge would mangle the fleshy root, make it jagged, and so prevent a complete adhesion) cut off a slice from the upper part of the root, making at the bottom of the part so cut a ledge whereon to rest the graft; this is recommended because you cannot tongue the graft as you would do a wood shoot, and the ledge is useful in keeping the cutting fixed in its place while you tie it; next cut the scion sloping, to fit, and cut it so that a joint may be at the bottom of it, to rest on the aforesaid ledge; a union may be effected without the ledge, provided the graft can be well fixed to the tuber, but the work will not then be so neat. It is of advantage, though not absolutely necessary, that a joint should be at the end of the scion, for the scion will occasionally put forth new roots from that lower joint; the stem is formed from the upper joint. I therefore procure the cuttings with the two lower joints as near together as possible. After the graft has been tied, a piece of fine clay, such as is used for common grafting, must be placed round it: then pot the root in fine mould, in a pot of such a size as will bury the graft halfway in the mould, place the pot in a little heat in the front of a cucumber or melon frame, if you chance to have one in work at the time; I prefer the front, for the greater convenience of shading and watering, which are required. A striking-glass

E

may be put over the graft or not, as you please. In about three weeks the root should be shifted into a larger pot, if it be too soon to plant it in the border, which will probably be the case; for, supposing the work were begun in March, the plant cannot go out till the end of May, so that the shifting will be very essential to promote its growth till the proper season for planting out shall arrive."

Nash, in *Loudon's Gard. Mag.*, vol. vii. p. 38, advises that " dry roots of inferior sorts be kept in a dormant state, for stocks; and, when the cuttings of the kind intended to be propagated are ready, single tubers should be taken from the dormant roots, and slit from the top two inches downwards; the scion then cut to a wedge shape, and inserted into the incision of the tuber; after which bind it well up with bass (matting). The grafts may then be potted into small-sized pots, and placed in heat."

Where fermenting materials, or the convenience of frames, greenhouses, or other protection during propagation, as above noticed, are not procurable; or, where the necessary time and attention cannot, or is not required to be, devoted to the means of propagation detailed above, the old entire roots may be kept inactive till May, and then planted out at once in the open border, where they are intended to flower; taking the precaution to cover them with a hand-glass, or other protection in bad weather; that is, when frosty nights or cutting winds prevail. Planted in this manner, the crown or eyes should not be covered; and care must be taken to prevent a superabundant supply of moisture. After the buds have pushed, and attained the height of three or four inches, slip or cut them off, (with a portion of the root attached if possible,) and place them *singly* in small pots in a light soil; or plant them in a southern border with a light soil, in the open air; and give due attention to shading and protecting them from the heat of the sun, or from intense cold. It may be well here to advert to the practice I have recommended of potting the cuttings *singly*, as I am well aware that some cultivators will place ten, twelve, or more cuttings, in one large pot: this, I presume, is done solely because it is imagined thereby to save trouble; but certainly a more mistaken notion cannot be conceived: for by which, I ask, is most trouble occasioned—by placing a number of cuttings in a pot, and after they have struck, potting them singly into small pots, or by simply potting them singly into small pots at once? surely it requires no argument to support the latter practice. It, however, may be alleged, that, should some of the cuttings not succeed, the trouble they have occasioned will be wholly lost; to which I reply, that if the cuttings are carefully taken off, and judiciously attended to, not one in a hundred will fail. The only shadow of an argument that can be brought forward against this practice, is that the cuttings, by being potted singly at first, will occupy more room in the house or frame, and this, at a season of the year when every inch of room is valuable; but this can only apply to the collections of nurserymen or florists where an immense number of plants is required, as I presume there are few gardeners or amateurs but can spare sufficient room to allow of their Dahlias being potted singly into small pots, a few weeks sooner than if they had first been placed more numerously in larger ones. I do not contend that this system will apply to all other plants; but with such plants as the Dahlia, it will save much unnecessary trouble, produce plants more speedily, and ensure much greater and more certain success, to place the cuttings singly into small pots as soon as they are taken off.

Another method of propagation in the open air, is to place the old entire roots in a warm situation, (a south border is the best,) and cover them, except the crowns, with old bark or light soil; observing to shelter them from frost, and other injuries to which they may be liable: when the buds have broken, and are an inch or two in length, the roots may be divided into as many parts as may be desired; taking care that each division has one or more promising buds on it. Again, if the roots are laid under the stage of a greenhouse, vinery, or peach-house, or even in a cellar or fruit-room, they will often break tolerably well; and may be twice or thrice separated, as well as afford shoots for cuttings.

Plants raised according to either of the last-mentioned methods, frequently grow stronger, and flower better, than those which have been raised earlier in the season by the application of heat. Under these circumstances, it becomes a question of great interest with the cultivator, whether heat is or is not necessary in the propagation of this plant. Of course where a large stock is required, heat is indispensable; but where the cultivator only wishes to obtain a few plants of each sort for his own garden, I am not prepared to say that he will not have finer plants and better flowers, without the application of any artificial heat in propagation. This opinion may, perhaps, be considered ridiculous and absurd by many eminent florists, but I appeal to every individual who has purchased plants from a nurseryman or florist, whether they have not been almost uniformly weak and slender, and have never proved such fine plants, or produced such good flowers, as those of his own raising. What then is the cause of this? simply and evidently, because the nurseryman or florist, in his anxiety to raise in a short time a great number of young plants, places them in *too high a temperature;* and thus renders them inferior to those which have not been so highly stimulated. I do not pretend to assert that Dahlias may be propagated most successfully, or that invariably the best results will accrue, from withholding artificial heat altogether; for to this it may be objected, that the plants raised without any heat will not produce their flowers so early in the season as those to which heat has been applied, and consequently that they will not arrive at perfection till the frost appears to destroy them: but this objection is by no means to be considered fatal, as in many instances it is totally inapplicable; and I do consider, that this subject is worthy of the most attentive consideration of every admirer of the Dahlia; not only because the plants and flowers may thus be improved, but because, if artificial heat could be dispensed with, a great saving of trouble and expense might also be effected. Before, however, I quit this subject, I will venture to affirm without fear of contradiction, that the less artificial heat is employed in the propagation of old and known sorts of the Dahlia, the stronger and more healthy the plants will be, the flowers finer, and of richer colours, and every part of the plant will appear more in its true and desirable characters.

There is yet, however, another system of propagating old varieties of this plant, which requires a brief notice; and this is, by cuttings taken off the plant in the summer season. This method is never employed except with such sorts as are extremely rare; and in all other cases it is wholly useless. To carry it into effect, cuttings are taken from the first lateral shoots that are produced, and the extremities of the shoots are always selected for this purpose, taking off the cuttings just below the third or fourth joint from the top; this done, place them singly in small pots, and keep them in a hotbed frame till they are struck, when they should be repotted into larger pots, and gradually but speedily inured to the open air; if they are taken off as early as possible in the season, and instead of being planted out into the open soil, are kept in large pots, and plunged into the bed or border, they will sometimes flower well, and form good roots before the frost appears; but in the beginning of October, if the roots are not considered sufficiently matured, the pots should be taken from the soil, and kept in a greenhouse or frame, till the tubers have arrived at their full growth. There is also a system practised by some cultivators, of taking off cuttings in the autumn, and, having struck them, preserving them through the winter in foliage, to be ready for planting out in the spring; but to this method there are many objections; and, except with very rare and valuable sorts, neither of these latter systems is worthy of adoption.

PLANTING OUT.

Having thus detailed the various methods of propagating the old and known varieties of this plant, and the treatment requisite to bring it to the state fit for planting in the open ground, I shall next notice the time and manner of planting out. The distance at which the plants should stand from each other, is a subject that requires some consideration, as it depends in a great measure on the taste of the cultivator; some persons desire a large number of flowers, merely to obtain a general showy effect, with little or no regard to individual merit; while others prefer such flowers as possess sufficient merit to be brought into successful competition with others, without reference to number. Where an uninterrupted display of flowers is the object, I cannot convey the directions for planting, to fulfil this aim, in better words than those of the late Mr. Sabine, which are as follows:—" Georginas (*Dahlias*) look best in a large mass, unmixed with other plants; in this plan of growing them, some nicety is required in the due distribution of the sorts, so as to have a proper and good admixture of colours, and particular care is taken to keep the tallest-growing sorts, either in the centre, or at the back of the clump, according as it is destined to be viewed, from one side only, or all sides; and to place the whole, so that there shall not be any unevenness in the general shape of the entire mass, arising from the irregular arrangement of individual plants, according to their respective heights. The roots should be planted three feet from each other every way; this distance will keep each sufficiently distinct, and yet so united, that the whole clump will have the appearance of an unbroken wood or forest of Georginas." To these remarks on this subject it would be superfluous to add any thing, further than that I fully agree with Mr.

Sabine, in considering that Dahlias look best when planted in a large clump by themselves; for a more striking or magnificent sight cannot possibly be imagined, than is presented to the view in a large and unbroken mass of Dahlia flowers, of every variety of colour. I should, however, consider that while the plants are placed three feet from each other in the rows, there should, according to this system of planting, be at least four feet left between the rows, to admit of the necessary operations of pruning and tying up the plants, and afford facilities for examining and plucking the flowers.

Where Dahlias are grown on either side of a walk in avenues, (which will have a very imposing appearance,) they may be planted about two feet and a half distant from each other; as in this case they can be attended to from the walk. To grow flowers for competition, the plants should stand at such a distance from each other, as to admit of a person walking at liberty between them, for the purpose of dressing, pruning, and otherwise attending to them. The best system for growing plants which are required to produce flowers for competition, is to plant them in slightly raised longitudinal beds, of about three or four feet in width, where only one row of Dahlias is intended to be planted, and six feet where two rows are desired; which latter is by far the better and most economical plan. Between these beds, there should be parallel walks, of from one to two feet in width, and the plants may thus be viewed, examined, pruned, or undergo any required operation, without treading the soil down closely about their roots, which is always more or less injurious. In the beds thus formed, the plants should stand three feet apart, if planted in single rows; and four or five feet, in beds with double rows; while the rows may be about three or four feet from each other. The ensuing season, they should not be placed in the same spot, but in the intermediate space, which should then be dug up, and formed into beds: this is of great advantage, for by constantly practising it, Dahlias will flourish in the same plot of ground for an almost indefinite period of time, without being subjected to any of the evils attendant on growing successively one species of plant in the same situation and soil year after year.

Having brought the plants forward in pots, and inured them so as to be capable of enduring the open air, they will now be ready for final transplantation. The time generally recommended for planting out Dahlias is about the latter end of the month of May; but not unfrequently does the cultivator find (especially in the north of England) that all his hopes are frustrated by an unexpected frost coming, and cutting off the whole of his plants, which before had appeared so promising. It is therefore much better to defer this operation till the beginning of June, when there will be little danger of the plants being thus mutilated. The holes for their reception should be made sufficiently spacious, and the soil reduced to a moderately fine state; the ball or roots must then be carefully turned out of the pot, observing to keep it as entire as possible; then remove the potsherds, &c. from the bottom, and place it perpendicularly on the soil, bearing in mind that the upper part of the roots should by no means be more than three inches beneath the surface of the ground. When this operation is performed, and the soil is placed carefully about the roots, give a little water for the purpose of settling the soil. For some time after planting out, it will be necessary to administer a small quantity of water in the evening of each day, after which a moderate-sized flower-pot should be placed in an inverted position over each plant, removing it in the morning when the weather is favourable. Should the heat of the sun be too powerful and cause the plants to droop, they may be effectually shaded by sticking a few branches of common laurel or spruce-fir in the soil, on that side of the plant which is most exposed to the sun. Throughout the whole period of their growth, attention must be paid to keeping them moderately moist about the roots; and, if water is not supplied by rain, it must be administered by hand, for a great deficiency becomes manifest if the roots are permitted to become too dry. It is necessary here, however, to caution against making them immoderately wet; for it has been before observed, that any superabundance of moisture has a most injurious tendency, inasmuch as it causes a diminution in the quantity, and deteriorates the quality of the flowers. Some persons prefer watering in the morning of the day, but I consider that the evening is decidedly the best time; as, at this season, the danger from the heat of the sun, attendant on early watering, no longer exists; and by covering the plants at night with a flower-pot, as before-mentioned, there can be no fear of their sustaining any injury from occasional slight frosts that may occur.

In excessively hot weather, to prevent the too rapid evaporation from the soil about the roots, a layer of moss, or old bark, is recommended to be placed on the surface of the soil for the space of about two feet round the stem; and this practice, besides assisting in the retention of moisture about the roots, is said to heighten the colour of self-flowers, but to prove injurious to tipped or variegated ones. The use of the above substances, although fully answering the purpose for which they are employed, should be had recourse to with great caution, as they afford a favourite place of resort for earwigs, and other vermin, which eat the petals, and otherwise disfigure the blooms and injure the plants. I have mentioned them, rather to show that they have been useful for the purpose of preventing excessive drought, than to recommend a further or continued application of them. To the use of rotten manure for this purpose, (or perhaps fresh cow-dung is the most suitable,) there can be no objection; for while the latter article is of a close adhesive nature, and thus proves unfavourable for the resort of insects, it is also efficient in keeping the soil cool and moist about the tubers; it should be liberally applied for the distance of two feet all round the base of the stem of each plant.

Some persons consider the application of manure-water calculated to make the plants stronger, and the flowers larger and better; but this system I beg to deprecate in the strongest terms; for while I allow that the plants may thus be rendered stronger,

I am fully convinced that it will totally destroy the quality and character of the blooms: my objections to this treatment may be seen more fully stated and enforced in the remarks on the immoderate use of manure, in a former part of this little work. It is true, that if water is administered to those plants which have manure placed round their roots, it will have the same effect, and, in fact, be precisely the same application as manure-water; but where manure is made use of in the manner above recommended, water may be wholly dispensed with; as the manure will of itself be sufficient to preserve a due quantity of moisture about the roots.

PRODUCTION OF VARIETIES.

I now proceed to notice the measures necessary to be used for the production of new and different varieties of this plant; and for this purpose, nature herself has provided a most simple and certain means, whereby a never-ending variety of sorts may be obtained: it is scarcely necessary to state that this end is accomplished by *seeds*. It is a matter of some disputation among cultivators, whether it is necessary to fecundate artificially the flowers from which the seed is intended to be taken, and various opinions are entertained on the subject: it is not, however, for me to decide which opinion is correct, and which erroneous, on this question; but I consider that artificial impregnation is by no means unnecessary, and I should decidedly recommend the practice of it, particularly as it is unattended with any particular trouble or difficulty, and may probably be productive of much good. For the purpose of procuring good seed, I should advise that plants of choice and esteemed sorts be planted solely for this end; and that the shoots should be pruned off as soon as they appear, leaving only a few of the uppermost ones: from these, the first flowers (which are never good) should be plucked off as soon as they appear; and then from twenty to thirty should be allowed to remain for the purpose required, and all others taken off as they appear: from the flowers thus left, the finest and best-formed ones should be chosen; and as soon as the disk begins to show itself, they should be covered with thin muslin, or gauze, to prevent any natural fecundation either by the bees or wind, from other and bad sorts. As soon as the florets expand, the pollen from other varieties, of opposite colours, may be introduced for two or three successive days with a camel-hair pencil; and as the florets continue expanding, this operation may as often be performed; taking care to keep the flowers covered with the before-mentioned or similar materials, till they are beyond the reach of cross fertilization by the bees, wind, or other casualties. Much has been said by different writers on the subject, respecting which row of florets is the best for performing this operation upon; but I am of opinion that this is an unnecessary and ridiculous cavil, and that it is quite immaterial which row is selected for the purpose; so that I should recommend that the whole of the florets be fecundated: in collecting the seed, however, the outer circle of seeds, which, being large, generally produce single flowers, should be rejected; and those of the extreme centre might also be discarded, as being imperfectly formed. It is scarcely necessary to add, that the flowers which have been thus impregnated should in some manner be marked, in order to distinguish them from those which have not been thus operated upon. I am aware, that some will consider the whole of these operations totally unnecessary; but if the person who practises them succeed in raising a greater number of superior new sorts than the individual who rejects and despises them, (which I feel assured will be the case,) he will be amply rewarded for the trifling labour bestowed. As soon as the seeds are properly matured, collect them on a fine day, and having dried them, it is advisable that they should be rubbed out of the heads, (otherwise they are apt to become mouldy,) and kept in a dry situation till the time for sowing.

About the middle, or latter end of February, sow the seeds in a light soil, in shallow pans or flats, and place them in a hothouse or hotbed frame, where they can be kept near the glass, and be freely exposed to the light. As soon as the seed-leaves are properly developed, they should be pricked out into other pans, at the distance of about an inch from each other, and kept in a hothouse or hotbed frame, with due attention to watering, shading, &c., till they have attained the height of two inches, when they may be potted singly into small pots, and gradually inured to a lower temperature till they are capable of enduring the open air; shifting them into larger pots when required, and especially continuing to keep them as near as possible to the glass.

It is unnecessary here to repeat the directions I have before given, and the methods I have before recommended, for hardening and otherwise attending to the young plants; directions for which may be found in a former part of this treatise, where propagation by cuttings is treated of. When the plants are brought to a proper state of maturity for placing in the open ground, they may be planted in compartments by themselves, according to the regulations before given for planting old and known varieties: they should be placed about three feet distant from each other, either way, to allow sufficient room for walking between them to examine their flowers; for, till a seedling shows its flowers, there are no means of ascertaining its qualities. Some persons, it is true, sagely pretend to foretell the colours of the flowers by that of the stem; but at present no rules on which any reliance can be placed have been deduced. Indeed, were it really possible to form a correct idea of what the colours of the flowers would be, I cannot imagine what advantage would result from it; for I have yet to learn that one colour is preferable to another, provided the colours are rich and clear; and even though this were the case, it is absolutely impossible to say whether the flowers would be double or single; so that I consider any attempts to ascertain the colours of flowers, before the flowers themselves appear, are wholly futile. I will, however, generally and briefly lay before the reader the opinions that are usually entertained on this subject:—Plants with wholly green stems, in many instances produce white flowers; those with whitish or light-coloured stems, may not unfrequently be seen with pale or blush-coloured flowers; and those with brownish, or purple-coloured stems, almost invariably produce the darker-coloured flowers.

After planting, the seedlings should be supported by placing a single stake to each plant; and treated precisely in the same manner as the old and known sorts. As soon as the flowering season commences, they should be visited and examined early in the morning of every day; for the colours may be better ascertained at this time: as, after the sun has shone upon them, the colours are often materially changed. Those plants which are not considered worth preserving, should be at once eradicated, that they may not exhaust the soil to no purpose; and those which prove good and valuable should not be suffered to blow immoderately, in order that the roots may retain more nourishment, and be better calculated to produce strong plants in the ensuing season. Many writers on Dahlia culture recommend that seedlings which are considered good should be taken out of the ground, potted in large pots, and placed in the greenhouse to continue them in bloom; but what advantages are to be derived from this mode of treatment they have not yet explained to us: certainly, where a seedling does not produce its flowers till the season is far advanced, it may be necessary to resort to this system, in order to obtain a more correct idea of its true characters; but even in this case, the great check it will receive from shifting will cause a manifest deficiency in the flowers, and the object desired to be accomplished will thus be wholly counteracted. There is, however, an obvious impropriety in subjecting those plants to this treatment, the characters of which have been fully ascertained: for such a course of proceeding must have a tendency to impoverish the roots; and the consequence will be, that, instead of the flowers improving and becoming finer in the ensuing season, (which is generally the case,) they will be far inferior; and the cultivator will be led to discard a plant which might have proved truly valuable, merely because it had been treated injudiciously. Under these convictions, I again urge upon my readers the importance of checking a further development of the flowers of seedlings, after their characters are known and determined; and I feel assured, that by such treatment, a considerable improvement will be apparent in all the characters of the flowers in the succeeding season. The properties necessary to constitute a seedling Dahlia worthy of notice will be hereafter adverted to, and I shall now take into consideration the different methods employed for training this plant.

TRAINING.

Many and various as are the systems by which this plant is trained, there is not one of them which can be said to possess the slightest advantage over another, further than that of more efficiently supporting the plant, bringing the flowers better into view, or distributing them more uniformly over a greater extent of surface: for all other purposes, the management of Dahlias, in this respect, depends entirely on the taste of the cultivator; some growing them for the purpose of having a rich display of flowers, others to produce fine individual specimens for competition, and many for the sake of having them trained in a peculiar and fancifully ornamental manner. The most natural and elegant method, and that which is more generally practised, is to train each plant timely and carefully to a single stake. Each stake should be strong, (larch-wood is the best,) and of at least an inch and a half in diameter; to enable it to sustain the plant during heavy rains, and strong rough winds. If the end which is to be driven into the soil be left rather obtuse, it will be less liable to wound the roots, if in its descent it should come in contact with them. To prevent this, however, it is advisable to put in the stakes at the time of planting. Each stake should be inserted perpendicularly, and as closely as possible to the stem; and to render it secure, it should be driven one foot and a half or two feet beneath the surface of the soil; leaving as much out of the ground as the ascertained height of the plant may be expected to require. As the leading shoot progresses, it should be secured to the stake with bass-matting; observing not to fasten the band tightly round the stem, but to leave sufficient space for it to grow to its natural size. If, however, the weather is such as to endanger the safety of the plant, unless it is firmly secured to the stake while yet in a growing state, it will be necessary to visit the plants regularly once a week, and change the band, leaving it as slack as shall appear safe and prudent: of course this practice may be discontinued when the plants have attained their proper size, as it will then be unnecessary. This system of training is almost universally practised where Dahlia flowers are grown for competition; in which case, as soon as the lateral shoots begin to appear, they are carefully slipped or cut off, and the plants are only suffered to retain the uppermost shoots, which then form a bushy and uniform head: by this practice, the flowers produced will be much stronger and finer, as well as more faithful in colour and form. Nor do the operations of the ingenious florist cease here, for he rightly concludes that the fewer the number of flowers the plant has to support, the finer those flowers will be in every respect: and, acting upon this theory, the flowers are removed as they appear, leaving only such a number as he expects will obtain sufficient support to enable them fully and perfectly to develop themselves. In adopting these principles, the shoots should invariably be taken off *as soon as they appear*, and the flowers be plucked *while in the bud;* for, if they are left till they are perfectly formed, the strength of the plant will have been exhausted, and the remaining flowers impoverished to no purpose. It is partly owing to the practice of such methods as this, that some persons usually ensure success when their flowers are brought into competition; but there are many other operations performed on the flowers by florists and others, before they are considered fit for exhibition.

It is not for me, however, to attempt to expose the trickery and cunning which are practised in preparing the flowers for public rivalry. It is much to be regretted that any unfair means should ever be resorted to; such as extracting those petals of a flower which are not perfect, and substituting others from different flowers; but this, and similar nefarious practices, are now so generally adopted, that it would be almost a hopeless task to attempt to abolish them. The most efficient means for effecting this purpose, would be for judges at Dahlia-shows to subject the flowers exhibited to the strictest scrutiny, and where any unfair deception was detected, not to allow the persons practising it to compete with others at all. The evils resulting from this dishonest practice are many and great; for instance, a person not skilled in the art of twisting, turning, and transposing the petals of his flowers, and otherwise artfully and unnaturally causing the blooms to *appear* perfect, brings a quantity of Dahlias to an exhibition, and, because the petals of his flowers (being natural) do not lie over each other in the requisite formal order, (though superior in other respects,) he has the mortification of seeing the prize awarded to an individual, who, perhaps, has not devoted half the attention to their cultivation that he has, but who has learnt the art of patching up his flowers, so as to make them appear good whether they really are so or not. Now, this should not be the case; and I am persuaded, that if the umpires at Dahlia-shows were critically and attentively to examine the flowers exhibited, such mean and paltry tricks might readily be detected and exposed. I am not opposed to the practice of adjusting the petals of flowers so as to dispose them in more perfect order, but I do protest against and strenuously reprehend the system of plucking out the petals and introducing others, with similar practices well known amongst Dahlia growers, as most iniquitous and unjust, and highly calculated to check and impede the progress which is now being made in the cultivation of the Dahlia; for, a truly honest and intelligent cultivator receives no encouragement to persevere in his assiduous and laudable efforts, but, on the contrary, is chagrined at finding himself outrivalled by such persons as do not scruple to make use of dishonest and unjust measures for preparing their flowers for competition. *Shading* will in many cases be found useful in growing flowers for competition; particularly of the white and light-coloured varieties, which are apt to lose the purity of their colour by being exposed to the rays of the sun; indeed, not only the sun, but heavy, violent rains, do much injury to flowers that are intended for exhibition: an excellent umbrella-like cover made of stiff paper, and affixed to a slender stake, (which is frequently used for shading carnation flowers,) will effectually prevent any injury to the flowers of Dahlias, if it is attached to the plant so as to cover the blooms intended to be preserved.

To return, however, to the subject of training. The method of placing three stakes to each plant at right angles, has been warmly recommended and practised by some cultivators; this system may certainly be advantageous in some respects, but it is objectionable in others. In training plants that are cultivated merely for their ornamental appearance, or the united beauty of their flowers, two prominent points are generally kept in view, *viz.* first, that of securely fastening and supporting every part of the plant, and next, that of keeping the materials to which it is trained out of sight, so that there may be one uninterrupted surface of branches, foliage, and flowers, presented to the eye. By the mode in question the plant is undoubtedly as secure, or perhaps more so, than when trained to a single stake; still, it should be remembered, that if the branches which are attached to the stakes should by any means be broken, the whole plant may be blown away by the wind; and when we consider that these branches are of a very slender and fragile nature, such an occurrence is not at all improbable: besides, as the stakes cannot be hidden without forcing the plant into an unnatural posture, and rendering it clumsy and unsightly, this system cannot be recommended for general adoption merely because some cultivators award it the preference. There are a great variety of iron frames and stands in use for training and supporting Dahlias, many of which are very neat and elegant in themselves; but when introduced into the Dahlia bed, and the plants trained to them, not only do they lose their interest, but the plant also loses its natural simplicity, and has a truly despicable appearance by the side of one trained to a single stake. They may, however, be used with a tolerably good effect, where solitary plants are placed out on an open lawn; although, even in this case, there is some danger of their being blown over by the wind: besides which, single stakes would have a much more elegant and natural appearance.

Some cultivators have a method of training Dahlias in the manner of espaliers, and in a few situations, plants thus treated have a very pleasing and interesting appearance, provided they are timely and cleverly trained; for I consider that the entire success of this plan depends upon fastening the branches, while young, in the direction they are wished to grow. They should be trained according to the fan system; that is, the branches should be diagonally disposed, equally on either side, and the centre filled up with the lateral shoots; in this case, the plant should be allowed to produce three or more stems from the root, and if there be horizontal as well as perpendicular stakes (forming a kind of trellis frame) for training the shoots to, the whole may be rendered more neat and secure. In situations where each side of a straight or curved walk could be devoted to a few plants of different coloured Dahlias, trained in this manner, the display of flowers would certainly be very rich, and have a very beautiful and striking effect; or, again, in cottage gardens, which front the road, plants trained in this manner would have a very showy appearance from the road. This mode of training, however, can only be pursued where a suitable situation is afforded, or where the taste of the cultivator may be favourably inclined to the practice of it, therefore it can be recommended only to such persons who may wish to adopt it for the sake of its novelty.

Another method, is simply to peg down the shoots as they grow, so as to have the appearance of a bed of dwarfs; but though this mode of treatment is gratifying to the taste of some individuals, I never saw plants so trained exhibit their flowers to the best advantage. Still, a bed filled with Dahlias trained in this manner, has a very pleasing effect among others in the flower-garden, and cannot be despised. To carry this system into execution, a bed of the flower-garden should be prepared for the purpose, and the plants turned out into it in the usual manner, and at the time before recommended; the number of plants requisite to fill the bed, must be regulated according to their respective heights; calculating what extent of surface a plant will occupy, when its branches are trained to their full length. The plants should not be allowed to produce more than one or two stems, and at the time of planting, these should be secured to the ground with a peg made for the purpose, and the shoots from them fastened down in a similar manner as they appear; in planting, the plants should be placed at such a distance from each other, as to allow of the extremities of the branches covering the whole of the stem of the plant next to them, so that the entire surface of the bed may present one uniform mass of shoots and blossoms; by this means likewise the roots will be kept moderately moist, without the application of water. I have seen plants of the Purple-Globe and the Springfield-Rival trained in this manner with very good effect, and I have no doubt that others would look equally well, if properly managed, and timely trained; but there is no system of training so well adapted to the habits of this plant, as that of reducing it to a single stem, and fastening it to a single stake; for this method is simple, secure, and elegant, and by it the flowers are exhibited to the greatest possible advantage. Indeed, this system can scarcely be termed *training*, for the plant grows in a perfectly natural manner; the stake merely being affixed to it, to support it during heavy rains, strong winds, or other casualties, which would either injure or destroy it.

PRESERVATION OF ROOTS.

The only points in the cultivation of this plant that yet remain to be noticed, are the measures necessary to be used for preserving the roots during the winter season. As the roots of this plant are seriously injured, and not unfrequently killed, if they are once suffered to be affected by the frost, it becomes indispensably necessary that means be employed to prevent its ingress to the place in which they are kept, and at the same time to preserve the roots from shrivelling, and protect the vital principle from all accidents. I shall, therefore, first consider the time and method of taking them from the soil, and afterwards the various ways of preserving them in a healthy condition through the winter, and yet in a perfectly dormant state. About the latter end of September, or as soon as frost may be expected, it is advisable that something should be placed round the base of the stem of each plant, and some judgment is required in choosing materials for this purpose. This operation is intended to answer the twofold object of preserving the roots from sudden attacks of frost, and of keeping them as dry as possible; to effect this it will be perceived that it is necessary to make use of some light and loose substance, and soil should by no means be employed. Some writers on the subject recommend pease-haulm, straw, or other similar materials; but these are objectionable, inasmuch as they have a very unsightly and slovenly appearance, and are liable to be scattered by the wind; it is therefore better to make use of old and coarse bark, which will effectually defend the roots from frost, and is not retentive of moisture. After the frost has visited the plants, and destroyed the leaves and branches, the stems should be cut down to within six or ten inches from the base, and the labels carefully secured to them with metallic wire; in this state they might be left in the ground during the winter, but that they would thus be liable to injury from excessive moisture, and it is much better to remove them from the soil at this season; for which purpose, advantage should be taken of the first fine and dry weather that occurs, and in the morning the roots should be taken up with great care, and left exposed to the sun during the remainder of the day; at night they should be removed into an open, dry, airy shed, and placed on shelves, boards, straw, or other material, where, with due attention to preserving them from frost, they may be kept till they are sufficiently dry for final removal to their winter quarters. When the soil about the roots is thus dried, all that can be removed without injuring them, should be taken off very carefully, and each tuber freed and cleared as far as possible.

There are two principal objects to be kept in view in preserving Dahlia roots through the winter: the first is, that of keeping the roots uniformly dry and dormant, and the second, that of preserving the vital principle unimpaired, that is, without injury from too great heat; and to accomplish these somewhat conflicting ends is a matter of some difficulty, and requires the exercise of care and skill on the part of the cultivator. Much depends upon the materials used for packing them in; and for this purpose either hay, straw, river sand, or dry mould, is generally employed; and perhaps the best of these, particularly for choice sorts, is a mixture of dry river sand and light dry soil. But, what is of much greater importance in the consideration of this subject, is the atmosphere and temperature of the apartment in which they are kept. Many persons have recommended, for the sake of saving trouble, that they should be placed under the stage of a greenhouse, where of course they would be secure from frost; but this situation is by no means adapted for the purpose, as they would thus be subjected to the drainage of the plants and other superfluous moisture in the greenhouse, which invariably accumulates in the situation just mentioned, and which would prove highly detrimental, and even fatal to Dahlia roots, by causing them to rot. The most eligible situation, and at the same time that which is best adapted to the required purpose, is a room which has a boarded floor; and it is immaterial whether it be over a shed, stable, or dwelling house, or whether it be on a ground floor, provided means are taken to exclude frost and damp. A room being provided, offering every desirable advantage, and precisely on the same principle as an apple or onion-room, take the roots (which have been previously well dried) into it, and after laying a thin stratum of sand, mould, or whatever may be selected to pack them in, over the floor of the room, place the roots as near as possible to each other, until the whole are deposited; after which, throw over them a slight covering of the same material, which should invariably be of a dry nature. But, if there be a greater quantity of roots than the room will contain, they may be piled upon each other in two or three successive tiers, provided a stratum of dry sand, or other proper material, and an abundance of dry straw, are placed between each layer, and a further quantity of dry straw (which is preferable to hay) strewn liberally over the whole. This practice, however, should not be resorted to, unless there is absolute necessity for it; as, if there is only one layer of roots, they may be examined at any time without any other trouble than that of removing the straw.

Mr. Loudon recommends that the choicest sorts be preserved in boxes, covered with very dry sand, and placed in a room, the temperature of which is never suffered to sink below 40° or 45° Fahrenheit. This is a safe practice; and, indeed, wherever they are stored, the temperature should on no account be allowed to fall below 36°. If there is any probability of frost entering the room, or damp arising to a dangerous degree, it will be necessary to introduce a little artificial heat, either by means of a brick flue passing through the room, or a common fire grate; but if neither of these can be conveniently procured, a small cast-iron stove, with a few lengths of pipe to carry off the smoke, would answer the purpose perfectly well. In this case, charcoal or coke should be used in preference to pure coal, as the former of these will burn more rapidly, and diffuse the heat more speedily and uniformly throughout the room; but great care must be taken, where heat is applied, not to suffer the temperature of the apartment to become too high, which would have a most injurious tendency, by causing the roots to shrivel. Where, however, the roots are judiciously and carefully packed, and a sufficient quantity of dry straw is employed to cover them, it is very seldom necessary to make use of fire heat, as all that is required in preserving the roots sound and healthy is to keep them from frost and damp; and some suitable place may generally be found which will afford ample protection in these respects. The apartment chosen for this purpose should always, if possible, be an upper one, and have a boarded floor; and where this latter is not the case, boards should be placed over the bricks or stoves, to lay the roots upon, in order to preserve them from the damp which is invariably generated by either of the above-named pavements.

PRESERVATION OF ROOTS.

A few years ago, the method of preserving this plant through the winter, in pits or cellars, (on the same principle as potatoes are usually stored,) was almost universally practised; but, in the present enlightened age, this mode has been wholly abandoned, except by a few prejudiced individuals, and such persons as possess a considerable stock of plants. Where this plant is cultivated on a very extensive scale, the common and less valuable sorts may be kept in a pit or cellar; but the rare and choicer kinds should by no means be thus treated. My objections to this system are twofold. In the first place, where Dahlias are pitted or heaped in ridges in cellars, the labels almost invariably fall from the plant (even though they should be attached to it with copper wire), on account of the damp which is constantly attendant on such a system; and, by this means, the various sorts become mingled in inextricable confusion; so that it is impossible to plant them out with any regard to uniformity or regularity of height, or variety of colour, in the ensuing season. The second objection is, that by this system, it is extremely inconvenient, and almost impossible, to examine the plants occasionally, so as to check any evils that may arise from damp or other causes; and that, consequently, many of the plants are frequently much injured by excessive moisture; and not a few wholly lost. These objections I consider serious, and therefore am decidedly opposed to this system, except with common or almost worthless sorts, which may be required for planting in the borders of shrubberies, or other obscure departments of the pleasure-ground. To preserve plants of the latter description, a very simple method is to place the roots in beds, on a hard surface, in any sheltered part of the garden, and cover them with six or eight inches of old bark, and they may thus be kept in tolerable safety through the winter. But, for esteemed and valuable sorts, no system of preservation can be said to offer equal advantages and security to that of placing them in a dry room: and in this situation, during the protracted period through which it is necessary to keep the roots in an inactive condition, they should occasionally be attentively and carefully examined; and if any indication of dampness, or mould, be discovered, judicious measures should be immediately resorted to, in order to eradicate the evil before it has produced its destructive effects. While prosecuting these examinations, it may also be discovered that the roots have not a sufficient quantity of straw, or other material, the labels may have become disarranged, or a variety of similar trifling matters may require attention, all which should be promptly rectified; and I am persuaded, that the cultivator will be amply remunerated for all the trouble bestowed, by the satisfaction of witnessing the roots taken out for propagation in the spring, in a perfectly sound and healthy condition, and fully prepared to resume those functions which have so long remained in a dormant state.

CHARACTERISTICS OF EXCELLENCE.

Having now furnished the reader with minute and detailed directions for the propagation, management, and preservation of this plant, with which some years' experience has made me familiar; it only remains for me to state the characters necessary to constitute a Dahlia worthy of notice, and to enumerate those particulars which florists agree in considering essential to any claim to merit or excellence. Under this head, I shall briefly notice the characters which a good plant ought to possess, and the points by which an approved flower is to be known; the former of these, however, (the perfection of the plant,) is of comparatively trifling importance, and may be considered only as a desirable accompaniment to a good flower: while the latter (the quality of the flower) is the prominent feature by which new sorts are tested and determined valuable or worthless. The characters necessary to constitute a good *plant*, may be comprised in three particulars: first, the general figure should be uniform and compact, that is, it should gradually enlarge from the lowest lateral shoots to the extremity of the highest ones, and should by no means manifest a straggling or rambling disposition or habit; secondly, it should be one that is disposed to blow freely, and produce a great number of flowers; and, thirdly, its blossoms should stand out clear from the foliage, on short and strong flower-stalks, so as to present themselves boldly and advantageously to view. These are the particulars which are generally considered necessary to form a good plant; but they are only valued as they are subservient to the more important consideration of the exhibition of the flowers to the greatest advantage: while the flowers, if good, are regarded as sufficient in themselves to render a new variety valuable without any consideration of the habits of the plant producing them. I will therefore proceed at once to the criteria by which the merit of the *flower* is determined. Those flowers that are large, of a brilliant colour, and even, so far as the general observer can determine, of a perfect form, are frequently considered unworthy of notice by those persons who are well acquainted with the characters necessary to constitute a good flower; so that it is important that this subject should be distinctly and properly understood. There are certain qualities which every flower must possess before it can be brought into successful competition with others of merit; and if the cultivator himself is not a competent judge, the flowers should be submitted to the inspection and scrutiny of a person well versed in the established rules: these rules, or criteria, are universally acknowledged and adopted by all Dahlia growers, and not left to the caprice of any individual, or the decision of any particular societies in their local districts; so that they are regarded as permanent, and beyond the reach of alteration, or the capability of improvement. This is of great importance; as, by submitting a new

Dahlia to the test of these established rules, its qualities may at once be ascertained, and it may accordingly be preserved or rejected.

The leading points, or tests, by which every flower intended for competition must be judged, are three, *viz.*; form, colour, and size; and these points are all dependent on each other in such a manner that, where a due degree of excellence of either of them is wanting, the flower is considered defective and unworthy of further attention. *Form* is certainly the most important feature, and is understood to apply solely to the shape of the petals and flower; whether the petals are perfect or imperfect, or whether the flower is filled up in the centre with good petals, or is deficient in this respect; and whether the outline of the flower be circular or broken. *Colour* is of comparatively minor importance; for a self, or flower of one colour, if well proportioned in other respects, will generally be acknowledged superior to one of finer and more varied colours, which is defective in form and size: if, however, colour be taken into consideration, it should, in flowers of one colour, be bright and clear, without breaking or running; and, in striped or tipped flowers, the colours should be uniformly distinct, and free from clouding, running, or blotching. *Size* is of much importance in flowers possessing the other requisite qualities; but where the size is the only recommendation, that is, when a flower has the advantage of being large, and is still deficient in the particulars of form and colour, it is at once rejected, as being unworthy to be brought into competition with others of decided and acknowledged merit in the latter respects. I shall, however, endeavour to condense, under separate heads, the particular characters which are universally admitted to constitute a good flower with regard to the three leading features before named.

1. *Form.*—The form of a Dahlia flower, when viewed from the front, should present one unbroken external circle, without any irregularity arising from the imperfect development of the petals, or from a want of conformity in their shape or disposition; each petal should approach as near as possible to a circular figure, without the slightest disposi-

tion to be pointed or acute, but perfectly round at the extremity, and very slightly concave; but by no means so much so as to expose any part of the under side of it to view. This form is said to be illustrated in the most perfect manner, by the flower which is termed the "Springfield-Rival," the petals of which are certainly very slightly curved; but I consider that this flower, though so perfect in this respect, is defective in not being of a perfectly hemispherical figure. Any irregularity in the shape of the petals, such as their being notched, quilled, convex, or too much concave, pointed, &c., is at once sufficient to render the flower unfit for public exhibition and competition; and beside being of a perfect and uniform shape, the petals should lie over each other in the most precise order and regularity, otherwise the flower will be defective in its general form and appearance. In some full-blown flowers, the eye or disk is evident, and no flower can be brought into competition, with any chance of success, when it is thus defective. I cannot attempt to account for this deficiency; it is, however, certain that some flowers have a greater tendency to exhibit their eyes than others; and though in many cases it may be caused by the central petals falling back from their natural position, on account of the flowers having been expanded for a great length of time, yet I presume that it is not irrational or ridiculous to suppose, that it may be attributable, in some measure, to the poverty of the soil in which the plants are grown; for, it is a well-known fact, that most double flowers are unnatural and monstrous productions, caused chiefly by cultivation in a highly nutritive soil; so that it is reasonable to surmise, that where the petals assume their natural form, and appear in the character of florets, it may be owing to the want of sufficient nourishment from the soil in which they are placed, to produce perfect petals. I do not by this supposition intend to contradict what I have before observed, with regard to the injurious effect which too much manure will produce upon this plant, but merely suggest, that an extremely poor soil may have a tendency to cause the disk of a Dahlia flower to exhibit itself in such a manner, as to render it unfit and unavailable for competition; so that it is advisable to avoid either extremely poor or highly nutritive soil, both of which are more or less detrimental. If a flower does not present a perfectly hemispherical figure when viewed from the side, or is not precisely the shape of either half of any globular body, it is imperfect; and in proportion as it deviates more or less from this form, it is in the same degree defective; for a flower may be too prominent, or too flat in the centre, either of which is a manifest deficiency.

2. *Colour.*—The colour of a flower, whatever it may be, should be rich, clear, and distinct, as has before been mentioned; variegated flowers, such as the York and Lancaster, (the leading seedling at the Sheffield Dahlia-show last season,) should have the stripes of each colour definite and clear; that is, one colour should not mingle with or merge into another, but the edge or boundary of each should be preserved distinct, and there should be no spots, irregular blotches, or cloudings.

3. *Size.*—I cannot attempt to prescribe rules for size, neither is it at all necessary or desirable; for I consider that a flower cannot be too large, provided it is well and correctly formed, and the colour perfect and agreeable; these characters, however, are very generally deficient in large blooms, which are usually too flat, instead of being prominent in the centre, and of a hemispherical figure; the petals are likewise generally coarse and irregular, and the colours are seldom rich and clear. But where there are none of these imperfections or deficiencies, large flowers are decidedly preferable to small ones; and, if perfect in other respects, the larger the flowers are, the greater success will attend them when brought into competition, and the more valuable will be the sorts that produce them.

CONCLUSION.

I HAVE thus endeavoured to give my readers a general outline of the particular characters a good Dahlia must possess; and having conducted my little treatise nearly to a conclusion, while I find much cause to regret that the task has not fallen into abler hands, who would probably have treated the subject in a more popular and acceptable manner, I feel some little gratification in asserting, that the whole of the remarks made, and the regulations laid down or proposed, have not merely been confirmed by other and higher authority, but are the result of many years' experience in the cultivation of this plant; which, I flatter myself, has not been altogether useless or lost.

CONCLUSION.

It may appear desirable to some, that a select list of the choicest named sorts now in cultivation should be affixed to this little work, with the current prices at which each may be obtained; but had this been done, and a long list furnished, (which would occupy many pages of this work,) such is the almost endless multiplicity of sorts, such the fluctuating and inconstant prices at which they are sold, and such the numerous additions that are constantly being made, that should this little treatise be favoured to continue in circulation a few years hence, my readers would justly blame me for encumbering its pages with what would then, most probably, be wholly useless; so that I at once abandoned the idea of attaching such a list; more especially as printed catalogues of the most esteemed sorts are every year appearing from the more eminent cultivators, containing every necessary and desirable information, with respect to colour, height, and price. It is conjectured, that the number of named sorts or varieties of this plant now in cultivation, exceeds one thousand; and, from such an immense number, it is obviously impossible to give even a select list of any value, with the price at which each is sold; but, as a general rule for purchase, it may be observed, that the newest and best varieties seldom exceed a guinea per plant, and very frequently not more than half that sum; these, in the course of one or two years, may be usually obtained for one-half, one-third, or one-seventh of their original cost; and after the third or fourth year, the price is still further reduced. This is one great reason why the Dahlia is so universally cultivated; and if any further inducements are necessary to bring it into still more extensive favour, it surely only requires to be seen flowering in perfection, to excite the admiration of every individual, whose taste is not so far vitiated as to gaze with indifference and coldness on the most pleasing and delightful objects, which Nature, ever charming, ever lovely, is continually presenting to our view.

THE END.

LONDON:
BRADBURY AND EVANS, PRINTERS,
WHITEFRIARS.

PUBLISHED BY WM. S. ORR AND CO.
AND W &. R. CHAMBERS, EDINBURGH.

HAND-BOOKS FOR THE PEOPLE.

Price 1s. 9d., the Third Edition of
THE HAND-BOOK OF GARDENING.

Price 1s. 3d.,
THE HAND-BOOK OF AGRICULTURE.

Price 2s.,
THE HAND-BOOK OF BOTANY.

Price 1s. 9d.,
THE HAND-BOOK OF NATURAL PHILOSOPHY.

Price 2s.
THE HAND-BOOK OF USEFUL MEDICINE.

Price 2s.,
THE HAND-BOOK OF COOKERY.

In the Press.
THE HAND-BOOK OF DOMESTIC CHEMISTRY.

"Capital little books. In the 'Hand-Book of Plain Botany,' the author walks into the fields, and plucks a primrose; he then dissects it, analyses its parts, scientifically describes them; and from this plain and simple beginning, lays the foundation of botany on so clear and sound a basis, that nothing, save a little care and attention, seems to be required from the student to master the elements of this pleasant study. The 'Hand-Books of Gardening,' and of 'Allotment Agriculture' (the former a new and much enlarged edition), are done with equal skill, but have more of a practical aim. The names explain the subjects of each: the mode of treatment is, first, to exhibit the science of the pursuit by unfolding the principles and causes which govern or regulate the growth of plants; and, secondly to detail the practice so far as it can be taught by books. The book on Gardening is intended for all classes; that on Allotments, for the poor. The execution of both—indeed of the whole three—is not only skilful, but has much of the ease and spirit of originality."—*Spectator*.

Price 7s., illustrated with Woodcuts of Birds, Cages, &c.,
A NEW EDITION OF THE

NATURAL HISTORY OF CAGE BIRDS;

THEIR
MANAGEMENT, HABITS, FOOD, DISEASES, TREATMENT, BREEDING,
AND THE METHODS OF CATCHING THEM.

BY J. M. BECHSTEIN, M.D.

"A very delightful book of its kind. . . . . . It seems to us an indispensable book for the bird-fancier."—*Spectator*.

PUBLISHED BY WM. S. ORR AND CO.,
AND W. & R. CHAMBERS, EDINBURGH.

PUBLISHING MONTHLY, PRICE SIXPENCE,

THE MAGAZINE OF DOMESTIC ECONOMY.

The object of this Periodical is to afford good and practical information upon all subjects connected with Domestic affairs, or which can be said to influence, in any way, the welfare of Society. It is not now necessary to detail the principles or plan of the work, as the numbers already before the public will furnish the best explanation on these points. That the projectors have not altogether mistaken the mode of accomplishing the object they had in view, is proved by the large and increasing circulation of the Magazine; and having every encouragement to persevere in their endeavours, the public may be assured that no pains will be spared to render the work practically useful in every department of Economy. Two Volumes were completed in July last, and may be had, price 6s. 6d. each, neatly bound in cloth, and containing copious Indexes. A Volume will be completed every year; and the Work will eventually form the most valuable compendium of USEFUL things in the language.

"We really do not know of a family, from that of the 'squire who keeps his town and country residence, to that of the tradesman and small farmer, to which it would not be of advantage to introduce this useful periodical. In some department or other of each of their domestic concerns, it will be sure to recommend something which will add to their comforts, improve their management, and benefit themselves."—*York Herald.*

"One of the best, because one of the most practically useful, little books that has fallen in our way. Replete with knowledge of the very best description, and sold monthly at a price which will enable every family to possess it, we warmly recommend the work to our readers."—*John Bull.*

"The characteristics of this valuable little work are utility and cheapness. It contains, within the compass of a few pages, more available directions for the management of a household, more plainly points out the beneficial employment of means, and economises in a greater degree both time and money, than works of ten times the size, and twenty times the price. It is a really good and useful companion to the housekeeper or head of a family."—*Bristol Gazette.*

"There is much, very much, of useful information in this magazine. It is intended to supply a void in our periodical literature, and to do for the domestic economy of our families that which other periodicals do for science, the fine arts, and general literature. Useful, rather than amusing, articles abound in its pages; and it will be found a valuable auxiliary in the family circle."—*York Chronicle.*

"This magazine is likely to be quite a treasure in families. The recipes alone are well worth the money."—*Liverpool Mercury.*

Printed in Great Britain
by Amazon